CW00642540

Too
Late

Kathryn Kuhlman

Never Too Late

BETHANY FELLOWSHIP, INC.
Minneapolis, Minnesota

Never Too Late
by Kathryn Kuhlman

Library of Congress Catalog Card Number
75-32235

ISBN 0-87123-397-5

Copyright © 1975
Kathryn Kuhlman Foundation
All Rights Reserved

DIMENSION BOOKS
Published by Bethany Fellowship, Inc.
6820 Auto Club Road,
Minneapolis, Minnesota 55438

Printed in the United States of America

Contents

Never Too Late

1

"I Had Begun to Die"

The great American humorist, Robert Benchley, once stated, "Life begins at forty." Yet it was in my fortieth year that I began to die. Not rapidly or all at once, which is a beautiful way to die, but bit by bit. Slowly, across the next seventeen years, my body stopped living—each section dying with agonizing pain.

I first noticed it one afternoon in my downstairs office at the Boysen Paint Company in Emeryville, a suburb of Oakland across the bay from San Francisco. I was almost a fixture at Boysen, having worked as a printer and typesetter for many years. It was my job to print all their letterheads, catalogs and paint-can labels. Behind my desk were the two big multigraph machines. In front of me was a big tray of lead type characters.

This particular afternoon the copy girl had just carried a bundle of newly printed labels upstairs. I picked up my tweezers and reached into the tray for some extra fine type. But something was wrong. It was almost imperceptible, yet my eyes were blurred and my hand was shaking. I had to stab at the type with my tweezers in order to pick it up. At the same time, I noticed a strange numbness in my hands and legs. Being a woman of great re-sourcefulness, I was often assured by my husband that there was no problem I couldn't solve . . . yet somehow I sensed this tiny thing, this shaking of my hands, this blurring of my eyes, this strange numbness, was far bigger than anything I had ever faced before.

Something had moved into the office. Even the bright California sunshine which had been streaming through the window seemed to turn gray. It was an invisible presence, dark and evil, which seemed to settle upon me. I dropped the tweezers.

"Mary, mother of God, what's wrong?"

Little did I know it was the beginning of seventeen years of hell on earth. Seventeen years of dying. Seventeen years of agonizing pain, dismal loneliness and unspeakable depression. At forty years of age, I had begun to die.

A year passed. Then two. I had been to half a dozen doctors in the Bay Area. One doctor said I had hepatitis. He put me to bed and treated me for inflammation of the liver. Another said I suffered from spasms of the esophagus. I was given more treatment, accompanied by three weeks in the hospital. A third doctor recommended gallbladder surgery, which I had. Then there were problems with bladder and bowel control. More surgery. Also unsuccessful.

Angelo, I call him "Ang" for short, was a supervisor at the Alameda Naval Air Base. Few men ever loved a woman like Ang loved me, which only increased the intensity of his frustration. Every few weeks he would come home and say, "I heard about a new doctor. Let's try him. Maybe he can help." We kept looking and hoping.

One doctor prescribed glasses for my double vision. Another said the numbness in my hands was caused by poor circulation. Yet my condition only grew worse.

One day I fainted at work. Two of the girls helped me to the women's lounge where I rested on the sofa until the dizziness disappeared. While I was resting, two girls from the marketing department came through the room. I couldn't help but overhear their conversation.

"Something ought to be done about these people who come to work drunk," one said.

The other snorted, "She was so wobbly she could hardly keep her feet under her."

That night I told Ang I was going to leave my job. Actually, I had been looking for an excuse to quit anyway. Rosemary, our daughter, was married and our two sons, Arthur and Don, were both working. Besides, Ang and I had long wanted another child. We agreed this would be a good time for me to quit work and adopt a baby boy. If, as one of the doctors had suggested, all I had was frayed nerves, then the change of pace might be just what I needed.

It turned out I needed more. Far more. Several weeks after little Eugene arrived, Ang went with me to the grocery store. Waiting in the check-out line, I suddenly grew dizzy and had to slump against Ang for support. As the line inched forward I found I could not pick up my feet. I had to force them to slide across the floor. I was scared!

I heard someone behind us talking. "Disgusting," she said. "This early in the morning and she's already hit the bottle."

I felt Ang stiffen. I didn't want him to make a scene. I tried to say something but the words wouldn't form. I could almost feel his blood boiling as he turned and faced the two elderly women, his balding head scarlet with fury.

"She's not drunk," he said through clenched teeth. "She's sick."

They flushed and hastily decided they needed to get another loaf of bread. I was so embarrassed. Ang was still steaming as he helped me out to the car. I told him it didn't matter. But it did. It mattered deeply.

2

"I Suspected It —
Now I'm Sure!"

Ang suggested more doctors, but I was tired and discouraged—nothing seemed to help.

"I'm fed up with doctoring and hospitals," I argued with Ang. "All I want is to be left alone."

Ang never let up, however. Eventually, he wore me down and I consented to see a specialist in internal medicine.

"There seems to be something wrong with your nervous system," the doctor said following an extensive examination. "I'm recommending you to a top neurologist in San Francisco."

I wound up in Presbyterian Hospital for a month. Part of that time I was under the care of a psychiatrist. Still no diagnosis—just an endless treatment with drugs. I finally called Ang to come and get me, and to take me home to be with the family.

Two weeks later, after a quiet supper at home with Ang and Eugene, I got up from my resting place on the sofa to help Ang with the dishes. He cleared the table while I rinsed the plates in the sink. Ang stuck a salad plate under the running water. Screaming out, he dropped the dish in the sink.

"How can you stand that water?" he cried, nursing his hand. "It's scalding!"

"What do you mean?" I asked, sticking my hand back under the faucet. "It doesn't even feel warm to me."

Ang grabbed my hand and pulled it out of the water. I was horrified. The flesh was an angry red color. Burned! Yet I hadn't even felt it.

"That settles it," Ang said. "You're going back to the doctor before you kill yourself."

"No more doctors," I argued. "They can't help."

The next weekend my mother and father, who lived in Oakland, were visiting us. Ang told my mother about the scalding incident and asked her to exert additional pressure. Mom watched helplessly as I stumbled around the house groping for walls to support myself. She insisted I call the San Francisco doctor again. I finally agreed.

"There is nothing I can do, Mrs. Burgio," he said. "I suggest you commit yourself to the state hospital."

"Doctor," I said angrily, "I'm not a mental case. I just can't see very well and my legs don't work correctly."

Mother wanted to know what the doctor said but I wouldn't tell her. When Ang came in that night, he asked also.

"Don't mention doctors to me again!" I shouted. But where else can you turn when your body is falling apart? The church? My church said they believed in miracles but no one had ever seen one. So it was back to the doctor again.

Three weeks later I noticed the middle finger on my right hand was red and swollen. Ang took me to a new doctor on Mac-Arthur Boulevard. He lanced the finger so it would drain and then, after finishing with the bandage, turned to me.

"Is there something else wrong, Mrs. Burgio?" he asked.

I was hostile. "No, why?"

"Well, if I had treated a normal patient the way I treated you, she would have been screaming in pain. You didn't seem to feel the pain at all."

"Well, some doctors tell me it's mental. Others say there is something wrong with my nervous system. Who knows?" I shrugged and started out the door.

"Could I give you a physical?" the doctor said, tapping his stethoscope in his hand.

"Forget it. There's no more money."

"It won't cost you a cent. I want to do this for my own satisfaction. Let me put you down for a physical."

I sighed. "Okay. I guess one more examination won't hurt."

The finger healed slowly and I had to

return twice before my scheduled appointment. Each time the doctor asked questions about my condition. I knew he suspected more than he was saying. Then the day before I was scheduled for the physical, the bottom fell out of my life.

Ang went to work early as usual. Little Eugene, who was about two years old, came running into the bedroom and began pulling on the covers. "Up, Mama," he said, "up, up."

I yawned, put my feet over the side of the bed and stood up—or at least I tried to stand up. Instead my legs gave way under me and I fell heavily to the floor. I wasn't hurt since the carpet cushioned my fall, but when I tried to stand up, nothing worked. My legs were useless—paralyzed. My arms were almost as bad. I was helpless.

I finally managed to turn over on my stomach and wriggle out into the middle of the bedroom. Eugene was standing beside the dresser, staring. "Mommy's just playing a game," I whispered, not wanting to alarm him. "You be the horsie and lead the way and Mommy will follow you." And then I began the slow, laborious crawl from the bedroom down the hall and into the family room. My hands would not work so I had to move along with my elbows and hips. Eugene was busy enjoying the new game and was oblivious to my pain.

It took ten minutes to make the trip to the family room. By then I was totally exhausted. I tried once again to get to my feet, but my muscles were useless. I couldn't even reach up for the phone to call Rosemary.

Then, to my horror, I saw Eugene open the sliding glass doors and toddle out onto the patio. He was heading toward the wrought iron gate which led to the busy street. I called to him but he was already outside, toddling across the patio in his pajama top and diaper. I cried out but my voice broke and faded. I started to crawl after him.

The wrought iron gate that separated the patio from the street was open. By the time I reached the patio, Eugene had disappeared. I kept crawling, pushing myself across the rough concrete on my elbows and hips with nothing under me but my thin pajamas. The feeling of panic swept over me as I heard the cars on the busy boulevard.

"Dear God, please help me. Help me!"

But the words were lost in my sobs. I could go no farther. I collapsed in the middle of the patio, hands reaching toward the wrought iron gate which hung open on silent hinges.

The clock inside was striking 11:00 when I looked up and saw Eugene coming back through the gate. "Up, Mama, up."

I tried to move, but it was impossible. If I could only make him understand. I tried to talk, but only hoarse tremors came out. Then I felt it. A sadistic demon seemed to grip my body, ready to begin his fiendish torture. The muscles in my upper back trembled as they began to pull my shoulder blades together. "Dear God, what is this?" I cried. Then in a sudden flash of pain, I felt my neck snap back. My shoulders wrenched as though caught in a devilish vise. I began to gag as my head was forced backward toward my spinal column. I vaguely remembered hearing my mother talk about a child that once had convulsions, but I never dreamed it would happen to me or that it would be like this.

Finally, the spasms ceased and Eugene mercifully disappeared into the house. I was alone with my tormentor.

For five long hours I lay on the patio, helpless in the blazing sun. Like a worm dug from the soft earth and dropped on hot concrete, I could only squirm in pain, gasping for breath. I tried to cry out but my voice was hoarse and raspy.

"Please God," I begged through my desperate tears, "let somebody come to help me."

It was around four o'clock and as though in answer to my prayer, my friend, Anne Kennedy, was standing at the gate. "Marion, I've had you on my mind all day. What are you doing there on the ground?" she cried. As she took a closer look and saw my distorted face, I rolled my eyes in pain, making odd sounding noises in my throat.

She gasped and ran into the houe to

call Ang. At the same time, my oldest son, Arthur, arrived home from work. "Art, your mother! Hurry! Hurry!" I heard her say. Ang arrived very shortly and the two of them took me to the doctor's office on MacArthur Boulevard. Ang carried me very gently through the waiting room and into the small examining room.

I could hear the doctor's voice. "I suspected it. Now I'm sure. Multiple sclerosis."

The nurse gave me a shot for pain and treated the raw, skinned places on my body. Ang and Art took me home but I slept fitfully that night. Ang stayed home the next day and Art arrived in mid-afternoon with a huge, antiquated wicker wheelchair he had picked up at the Easter Seal Foundation. I was able to eat a little bit of supper and afterwards, on my insistence, Ang took down the dictionary and read to me the definition of multiple sclerosis.

"A diseased condition marked by patches of hardened tissue in the brain or the spinal cord and associated especially with partial or complete paralysis, jerking muscle tremors and sometimes intense pain."

3

Helpless and Hopeless

Twice a week Ang or Rosemary took me to the Easter Seal Foundation for physical therapy. The MS was progressing rapidly. There were constant spasms. My face was so twisted and distorted I couldn't bear to look in a mirror.

As the months slipped into years, I lost track of the number of trips to the hospital. On one such trip, I had a cardiac arrest when the nurse was serving my lunch. If the nurse had not been in the room when it happened, I would have died. I remained in the San Leandro Memorial Hospital for a month. But even that faded in significance when compared with the horrible pain and the utter hopelessness of having an incurable disease. Another time there were three spinal taps plus heavy dosages of cortisone. Even after I was dismissed from the hospital, I had to return for physical therapy.

Over the years I was to learn that multiple sclerosis is a strange disease. It will take you right to the brink of death, back off and allow its victim a partial remission and then, without warning, send your body into horrible spasms.

One Sunday afternoon I told Ang, "I'm not going to sit in this chair any longer." But when I tried to walk with canes, my hands could not grip the handles. The same was true with a walker. The next week the therapist recommended Canadian Canes, the kind that strap around your arms. Later on, I was fitted with a leg brace as my feet were twisted so badly I had to walk on the sides of my ankles. But nothing was able to stop the creeping scourge of death which was slowly penetrating my fortress of life and strangling the living cells.

Ang employed a full-time housekeeper and eventually a daytime nurse. We moved from our home in San Leandro to nearby Walnut Creek so I could be near Rosemary. But nothing seemed to help. Eugene, who was now in the second grade, needed immediate surgery on his spine. The doctors performed a spinal fusion and placed him in a body cast where he remained an entire year. Later the two of us were in wheelchairs at the same time.

It was no surprise to me that I finally reached the stage where I cried out to God, "Why have you forsaken me?" The day had been filled with much pain. I had fallen twice and the side of my face was badly bruised. My nurse had to leave early and it just seemed that nothing would ever be right again. I simply could stand no more and began to weep, crying out to God to deliver me from this transgression.

I heard Angelo at the door and tried to get up but pitched over on my face, bumping against the coffee table on the way down. I felt my body begin to spasm—my throat tightened up and I knew I was choking to death. Ang found me on the floor, clawing at my neck and saying, "Aw . . . aw . . . aw . . ." He rushed me back to the hospital.

This time it was nine straight days of intravenous medication—something called achthar, a repository corticotropin injection. My body did not stabilize, however, and I had to remain in the hospital another four weeks.

It was not just the pain of the disease, however, which was killing me. It was the darkness of depression and loneliness. In the months that followed, I slipped deeper and deeper into the dark pit of despair. I knew the disease was incurable. Ang was having to spend every cent he made just to keep me alive. My old friends who used to visit me slowly drifted away. Who could possibly enjoy visiting someone so twisted and distorted, now unable to see or talk clearly, who at best could only drag herself around on crutches and utter slurred words? Besides, as many ill people do, I had become bitter and resentful. Even when

Ang tried to cheer me up, I would reject him with negative answers.

One day in the doctor's office I broke down. I was losing my hearing. I couldn't even comb my hair or feed myself. The saliva drooled out of my mouth and my muscles quivered in excruciating, painful spasms. I had no one to talk to but my husband, children and hired help. The State of California sent me a record player and talking books since I was unable to read. I was totally dependent upon others.

The doctor said, "Mrs. Burgio, there is nothing more that I can do for you. You are beyond medical help."

"I wish I were dead," I wept.

The doctor knew better than to show sympathy so he challenged me to make the most of every day.

"But I'm going to die anyway. Isn't that true?"

He looked straight at me and said, "Yes, eventually we all do, but you don't have to die in such unhappiness."

"But how can I find peace and happiness when my body is dying?" I asked.

He didn't have an answer for a question like that. He shook his head sadly and walked out, rather than show his own emotions.

When he returned, I apologized for my outburst and he gently said, "There is no need for an apology. You have every right to feel the way you do."

There were more trips to the hospital. The heavy medication caused an ulcer which began to bleed. Another time I almost drowned in my own saliva as the throat muscles which enabled me to cough were useless. From that time on, I had a respirator with me at all times.

4
Seed of Faith

It was a January afternoon when Ang called our priest from nearby St. John Vianney Church in Walnut Creek. I had been on the couch all day, convulsing and moaning in pain. Breathing had become more difficult and it seemed as if every heartbeat would be my last. The priest gave me communion and then anointed me with oil.

"I don't think she's going to make it," he whispered to Ang as he walked out. I turned my face against the back of the sofa and wept softly. I felt that now God himself had pronounced the death sentence!

In June our family received an invitation to attend the Golden Wedding Anniversary celebration of Fred and Helen Smith, former neighbors in Oakland whom we had not seen in eleven years. My enthusiasm for going out was at an all time low, but Rosemary convinced me I should go. "We'll make it a family affair," she said, "and it will please Daddy." I agreed to attend.

Helen, a striking woman with friendly blue eyes, was at the door with a warm welcome for all of us as Ang rolled me up the sidewalk in my wheelchair.

"Oh, Marion," she said as she bent over to kiss me, "I'm so happy you came. I just know you are going to be healed."

Puzzled, I looked up at Ang. Neither of us understood what she could possibly be talking about. However, during the evening Helen told us all about the miracle services held by Kathryn Kuhlman and introduced us to several priests and nuns from Holy Names College who told us about the charismatic prayer meetings they were having at the college.

Helen was very enthusiastic about this new dimension she had found in her religious life, but Ang and I just couldn't take it all in—prayer meetings, healing services, and what she called "the power of the Holy Spirit." Who is this Kathryn Kuhlman they are talking about? Miracle service. "What is a miracle service?" we asked ourselves. Little did we know that soon, very soon, we would have glorious answers to both questions.

We left the party feeling that somehow our friends had changed. Something— we knew not what—was different in their lives, although we could not analyze it. We drove home unaware of the fact that Helen's seed of faith had been planted and that our family would reap the marvelous harvest yet to come.

A few weeks after the party, my ulcer flared up and the MS exploded with all the fury of a hurricane after the eye of the storm. It was a Sunday morning when I felt the muscle spasms begin to ripple in my back. I could feel the spinal column begin to draw and before I could even cry out for Ang, the convulsion hit, drawing my shoulder blades back until they almost touched. My head was drawn backward toward my spine. I could not breathe. Gasping, gagging, I tried again to cry out to Ang who was in the other room. I felt myself falling forward out of the wheelchair, and then Ang's arms were cradling my twisted body, lifting me and placing me on the sofa. I felt the mouthpiece from the respirator being forced between my clenched teeth and the cool flow of the life-giving oxygen hissing into my lungs.

So it was back to the hospital for me. The long years of fighting for my life had taken their toll. My will to go on was all but gone. My vision was badly impaired, my hearing almost gone, and now the muscles in my throat had deteriorated to the point where I could not swallow food. The sad look on my husband's face was becoming too much to bear. I had arrived at the point in my life when I truly felt it would be better for everyone if the Lord would take me home.

It was during this time of deep depression that Helen Smith and another friend came to visit me at the hospital. While there, Helen asked, "Do you mind if I say a prayer over you?" I looked at Ang in puzzlement. He just shrugged his shoulders as Helen placed her hands on my stomach and began to pray softly. Her eyes were closed, her face tilted up, her lips moving quietly expressing words I was unable to understand. There seemed to be a soft glow around her as though a light were shining from the ceiling.

As she was praying, the big toe and the little toe on my right foot wriggled, and from far off I heard the sound of music. Everything had been distorted for so long, yet this music was clear— beautifully clear. It was the eerie, yet harmonic, sound of a beautiful choir accompanied by the gentle melody of stringed instruments.

I cupped my hand over my deaf ear and exclaimed, "Oh, Ang, I hear music! It sounds like a beautiful choir."

He licked his lips nervously and ran his hands through the white tufts of hair above his ears. "Uh, Marion, maybe. . ."

"No, Ang, I'm serious," I said strongly. "I hear a choir singing. I don't know the song but it's beautiful."

It was as though a radio had been turned on in my ear, but it was impossible for me to describe the beauty of the music to those around me.

Ang thought I was dying and having hallucinations, as the doctor had told him that it was only a matter of time.

Helen's face was radiant as she said, "Oh, honey, you are going to be healed. I just know you are."

She and Ang talked quietly for a few moments before she left, but I was caught up in the sound of the choir. I put my head back on the pillow and listened, unworried about the source.

I was released from the hospital two weeks later. The doctor told Angelo there was nothing more that could be done and it would be better for me to spend my last days at home. Three days after I got home, I received a card from Helen. Angelo read it to me.

Dear Marion:

Glad you are home again. Hope you are feeling better. You are going to be well again. Praise the Lord. Both of you will enjoy the tape I am sending you today. You will find great help and inspiration from it. Hold on to your faith and believe. In case you go to Kathryn Kuhlman's at the Coliseum, I'll be there in the choir praying for you. Accept your healing when the time comes. God bless you, dear. Remember, you are being healed. Get there early, about 3:30 p.m. Wheelchairs go in first.

Helen

"Do you understand her?" I said to Ang when he finished reading.

"Not really," Ang replied.

He examined the small cassette tape which had arrived in the same mail. "It's by Kathryn Kuhlman," he said. My hearing ability was so distorted at this stage that I could not get very interested in listening to a tape by Kathryn Kuhlman.

"I don't want to hear it," I said. "I don't know what's the matter with Helen.

I just don't understand all this stuff about
healings and Kathryn Kuhlman."

Five days later, on July 28, we received another card.

Dear Marion and Angelo:

The meeting of Kathryn Kuhlman's is
at the Coliseum, Tuesday, July 30. I hope
you're feeling up to going. Plan to get
there by 3:30 and they will help you in.
Later on it's terribly crowded. You would
never make it. Love and prayers,

Helen

Shaking my head, I put the card on the
table. After seventeen years of suffering
and the total failure of the medical pro-
fession to find a cure for my condition,
healing in a miracle service was just
more than I could comprehend.

"I'm not going," I said to Ang. "Helen
just doesn't realize how difficult it is for
me to get around."

The next evening, Monday the 29th,
the phone rang. It was Helen. I heard
Ang say, "Yes, Helen, I'm taking the
day off and I'm going to take Marion to
the meeting."

When he hung up, I began to cry.
"Please, Ang, I don't feel like going.

We've been through so much already. Why bother with this?''

Ang said not to worry about it, that we'd talk about it in the morning. But I insisted, "We've never been in a Protestant service before, Ang, and I don't want to go."

The next day was the worst day of my life. I was twisted far more severely than ever before. The thumb on my left hand was bent back behind the knuckles on my fingers. My hands looked like claws and I was shaking like a vibrator. Even before I got out of bed, I took three pain killers but they had no effect.

"I'm not going!" I cried.

Ang was firm. "We have nothing to lose, honey, Let's go see what it's all about," he said.

Since I could not dial the phone, I made him call Rosemary. He held the phone against my ear while I talked, or rather while I wept, into the mouthpiece.

"I'm not going to go. Tell Daddy I don't want to go. Please don't make me go!"

"Now, Mother," Rosemary said soothingly. "If for no other reason, you should make the effort for Daddy's sake. And, who knows, it just might be entertaining if nothing else."

"I don't feel like being entertained," I cried. "You know I can't see and what's the use of going when I won't be able to hear what's going on."

"Now, Mother, don't talk like that. Don't disappoint Dad, Mom. Go with him and as soon as you get home, call me and tell me all about it."

Ang tried to dress me but all my clothes seemed to choke me. He finally got me into a pajama suit and covered my shoulders with a soft, white sweater.

5

"You've Gone Bananas!"

Ang did not tell me until we came home that evening, but before we left for the Coliseum, he had finally reached the breaking point. He had stood by the breakfast counter in the kitchen and fervently prayed to our Lord Jesus. "I'm not asking for myself, Lord. I'm asking for my wife," he wept. "She can't go on like this. I'm asking you either to heal her, Lord, or take her home to be with you."

The trip to the Coliseum was horrible. I cried all the way, begging Ang to take me back home. When we arrived at the Coliseum, one of the ushers tried to help

Ang with my wheelchair and I went all to pieces.

"Oh, don't touch me . . . please don't touch me! I just want my husband to take care of me."

She moved back and stood by helplessly while Ang tried to calm me down. "They aren't going to hurt you," he said.

Finally, we were settled in the huge Coliseum surrounded by others in wheelchairs and on stretchers. Ang was on one side of me and a young boy, perhaps fifteen, was on the other side. He was sitting next to his father who was also in a wheelchair. The Coliseum was filling rapidly and the choir was rehearsing on the platform. Soon, every available seat was taken.

All around us were people in wheelchairs and on stretchers. I could not comprehend the amount of human suffering that had come together in that one place. Yet there was something else present— something intangible—HOPE. Everyone, or at least nearly everyone, seemed to have a glimmer of hope on his face. It was as though each person was straining for some unseen hand to reach down and touch him. My heart ached for them and I began to pray, asking the Lord to help them.

Suddenly, the choir began to sing again. This time the great crowd joined them. That song!!! It was the same song which had been running over and over in my head.

"Ang!" I cried out. "It's the song in my head . . . it's the same song . . . the same choir!"

"Shhh," Ang said, trying to calm me down.

"No, Ang, you don't understand. It's the same song I've been hearing since Helen's prayer."

Ang gave me a weak smile and to appease me, he turned and asked the woman next to him, "What's the name of that song?"

"Don't you know the most popular Christian song in the world?" she asked. "It's called HOW GREAT THOU ART."

All the people around me seemed to have their arms raised as they sang. I asked myself, what kind of meeting is this anyway? I looked over at Ang and even with my double vision, I could see he had his arms up also.

"What are you doing?" I asked.

Ang smiled. "Well, everybody else has their hands up so I put mine up, too. It feels good to sing this way. I like it."

I wanted to scream. Everyone seemed so happy—even those in wheelchairs—yet I remained miserable and thoroughly confused.

I felt Ang's hand on my arm. "Here she comes. This must be Kathryn Kuhlman."

I strained to see, but my eyes simply would not focus on the platform which was at least seventy yards away. All I could see was a bright glow—like an aura. I knew it must be Kathryn Kuhlman.

"What's she doing?" I kept asking Ang. He tried to describe what was happening. She introduced certain guests. She told a few stories. There was more singing and then she began to speak. To me the sounds were all jumbled. The only word I heard plainly was BIBLE.

Then Ang said, "People are coming

Picture on the following two pages of The Coliseum in Oakland, California.

to the platform. They are falling down."

"What's wrong with them?" I whispered anxiously.

"I don't know," he said, "but when she prays for them, they fall down on the platform."

"Ang," I whispered louder, "I think we better get out of here . . . I feel funny."

He ignored me. His eyes were riveted on the platform.

Just then a woman, dressed in red, moved slowly down the aisle beside us. Her daughter was in front of her and her husband was walking behind her. As she got opposite our row, she dropped to the floor.

"Oh, dear God," I moaned, "help her." Her family was bending over her crying and trying to help her to her feet. I began crying also as I realized what my own family must have been going through as they had tried to help me.

When I looked up, I noticed another girl, a young woman, lying on a wheelchair stretcher farther down the aisle. She was dressed in a plaid suit but it was obvious her body, like mine, was the twisted victim of multiple sclerosis.

"Dear Lord, help her, too," I prayed.

Later, the woman in red passed by my wheelchair. She was beautifully transformed.

"Ang!" I cried out. "She's been healed!"

I could not tell all that was happening or even understand what was being said, but I knew it was the same woman. No longer was she hobbling and falling—she was almost running. Her face was radiant! The teenaged boy next to me said, "She has been healed of cancer."

It was then that the struggle within my own body began. Suddenly, my knees began to shake. I tried to hold them with my hands to calm the vibration but it was too much. Things were happening too quickly. My feet were being pulled out of the foot rests of the wheelchair and pressed against the floor. It seemed as though two great forces were at work within my body—one pushing me down and another pulling me up. I felt myself being lifted up, but the downward force was too great and I fell back into the chair.

Ang was alarmed at my movements and said, "Marion, what's wrong? What is happening to you?"

I couldn't answer, for I was literally being pushed right up and out of my wheelchair. It was as though the chains that had bound me had suddenly broken. I was on my feet! Standing! And as I stood up, my twisted hand just stretched right out. I couldn't believe my eyes—my hand was straight and normal! And I was standing!

Just as quickly as I had stood up, I began to walk. I didn't know where I was going or why—but I was on my way. Past Angelo. Past the place where Eugene was sitting. Down the aisle and toward the platform. Ang, in a state of shock, was following closely behind me.

The next thing I remember was Kathryn Kuhlman's voice. "You're healed, honey! Just walk across the stage," she said.

And then it dawned on me that I was walking back and forth, sometimes half running, in front of thousands of people. As Ang approached the microphone, Miss Kuhlman started to pray, but before she said anything, my Ang was slain by the power of the Holy Spirit! Of course, I didn't realize what was happening but, oh, what a glorious awakening the Lord had in store for all of us!

I was busy trying out my new feet and legs when Miss Kuhlman turned to me and before I knew what was happening, I had joined Ang—to fall under the power of the Holy Spirit. The peace and serenity that came over me is indescribable. I was very much aware of the reality of Jesus Christ and it seemed as though I was being bathed in God's love!

He was real! He had come to me! He loved me enough to minister to me personally and, glory of all glories, to fill me with His beautiful Holy Spirit!

I was perfectly content to stay right there on the floor, but somehow I got to my feet just as my son Eugene appeared.

"Mama, Mama!" he cried. "Now you are like all the other mothers."

"Do you mean you have never seen

your mama out of her wheelchair?" Miss Kuhlman asked.

"Yes, ma'am," Eugene replied.

"Thank you! Thank you!" I exclaimed to Miss Kuhlman.

Her face was smiling with joy. "Don't thank me," she said. "I'm just as surprised and happy as you. Thank Jesus. He's the One who healed you."

"I thought you were a farce," I said crying with joy. "I came only to please my family and my friends, Helen and Fred, who sing in your choir."

"Helen and Fred," Miss Kuhlman called into the microphone. "Where are you?"

"Here we are," they called from the choir.

I called back to them laughing and waving my arms with joy. Amazed at myself, I realized I could talk! My speech was normal! My eyes, too. I could see clearly! My legs were working! The pain was gone! I could breathe! Just as Helen had said it would happen, I had been healed!

As the three of us came off the platform, several people reached out to stop us, to speak to us, or to just touch us. Perhaps they thought the touch of God might rub off on them also.

I was literally floating through the crowd unaware that the Lord had yet another joy in store for me. I looked up and there was the girl in the plaid suit. Walking! She had been healed also! The tears started all over again. What joy to know that the two people I had prayed for—the woman in red and the girl with MS—had both been touched by God. And so had I. It was almost more than I could take.

When the service closed, we left through the wrong exit and wandered through the parking lot for almost an hour looking for our car. I walked the entire distance without any assistance. Even Ang was complaining about his legs being tired but I was strong and fresh.

The trip home was far different from the trip to the Coliseum. We sang all the way home. Sometimes, since we didn't know the words to the songs we had heard, we just made them up. What music!

Driving up Castle Rock Road, we saw our house. Every light was burning! "Oh, Ang, the Holy Spirit has fallen on our house, too. Look, all the lights are on."

In this case, however, the Holy Spirit had a little help. Our neighbor's friend had been at the service. She rushed out of the meeting and called to tell her I was healed, and she had turned on our lights to greet us when we arrived. It was a wonderful welcome!

The first thing I did was call Rosemary. "I'm healed!" I shouted.

"Oh, Mama, you've gone bananas," Rosemary chuckled.

"No, I'm healed. Listen to me talk. I can walk and I can see! I hear you perfectly. No more pain!"

"Listen, Mama, don't talk to anybody. You just go to bed and wait until I get there tomorrow."

"Honey," I laughed, "I can't even get angry with you. Here, talk to your dad. He was there too."

"Mama, just go to bed quickly. Don't tell anyone of this. I'll be over first thing in the morning."

I passed the phone to Ang, but even he could not convince Rosemary of the miracle. She would just have to wait and see for herself.

6

Life Begins at Fifty-Seven

The next morning, for the first time in ten years, I jumped out of bed and pulled open the window blind so the summer sun could come streaming into the bedroom. I headed for the kitchen to fix Ang some coffee while he dressed.

"Hey," I heard him shouting from the bedroom. "Come look at this."

Ang was standing in front of the mirror rotating his arm and shoulder. "You know how sore my shoulder's been from bursitis—even had to get a shot last week because the pain was so bad? Now look, I can put my shirt on without any pain. I'm healed, too!"

Half an hour after Ang left for work, Rosemary came rushing through the door. She had brought a friend—in case she needed help. I was in the kitchen drinking coffee.

"Praise the Lord!" I grinned.

She stood in the doorway with her mouth open. "Mother! Mother! What's happened to you?" she cried in disbelief.

She was like that for the next two hours as I told her everything. All she could do was weep and shake her head.

After she left, one of our neighbors phoned. "I'd like to speak to Marion, please."

"Honey, this is Marion," I laughed.

"Hey, who are you kidding? This isn't Marion."

"It sure is. I've been healed. I can talk now."

"You've what? I'll be right over."

In less than two minutes, she came bursting through the front door. She grabbed me around the neck. "Oh, thank God, it's true. You're healed!"

The passwords to the Burgios' coffee klatch that day were TEARS OF JOY

—everyone that came wept unashamedly in the presence of the miracle our Lord had wrought.

Monday morning I went to Doctor's Hospital for my regular X-ray appointment. The technician who had taken my X rays for the last two years looked at me strangely.

"You must be Marion Burgio's twin sister," she said. "I'm Betty."

I laughed. "No, Betty, I'm not Marion's twin. I'm Marion."

She grabbed me and pulled me into a side room. "What happened to you? Last week you were dying. Now look at you!"

"Do you believe in miracles?" I asked.

She shrugged her shoulders questioningly, but after I told her about my healing, she gasped, "I have to believe. Twelve days ago I had to put the straw in your mouth when I gave you the milkshake for the X ray. Now you're perfect!"

Just at that moment the door swung open and in walked the doctor. He stared at me but said nothing . . . just motioned me to get ready for my X rays. I undressed and leaned up against the slanted X-ray table. The doctor stood to one side watching.

"Don't you have any pain?" he asked.

"No," I said evenly.

"Haven't you had pain?"

"Oh, yes, constantly. But not anymore."

"When did the pain go away?"

"Last Tuesday night."

He asked no more questions, just kept turning me and snapping X-ray pictures. Through the thick glass window I could see Betty's face laughing and giggling.

Finally, Betty could take no more. She called out from behind the lead shield. "You remember Mrs. Burgio, don't you, doctor? She was here twelve days ago with multiple sclerosis."

The doctor's expression never changed. "You had an ulcer, too, didn't you?"

"I did but I don't have it anymore. It's healed."

"Hmmm, how do you know?"

"I don't have any more pain. I eat anything I want. I don't have to take medicine anymore."

"Have you stopped taking all medicine?" he asked, his eyes narrowing.

"I haven't taken any since last Tuesday night."

He cleared his throat as if he wanted to ask more but decided to keep silent. Motioning to Betty, he slipped off his lead apron and left the room.

It was sheer joy to be able to dress myself without assistance. I was so wrapped up in the realization of what I was doing for myself that I did not hear the receptionist when she returned. Her voice was quite firm. "You may go home now, Mrs. Burgio. I don't think we'll have to see you again."

More than anything, I wanted to tell the doctor about the miracle service but he was gone. I walked out into the hot August sun. A fresh breeze was blowing off the bay, the sky was so clear I could almost see into tomorrow. Everything was beautiful—to me, anyway. During my illness I had allowed myself to become bitter and seldom saw the day-to-day blessings the Lord heaps upon us all, but now everything was beautiful!

As I walked to my personal physician's office, I was wondering how he would react. After all, he had treated me for almost thirteen years and the last time he saw me, I was a completely helpless invalid, partially deaf and unable to see clearly or speak plainly.

He was standing in the hall talking to the receptionist when I entered the waiting room. I rang the buzzer on the desk and stepped back. He glanced up at me and started to turn away. My heart went out to him as he turned and looked again.

"Mrs. Burgio?" he asked timidly.

I just grinned.

"Where's your wheelchair?"

"I don't need it anymore."

"But your canes . . ."

"I've put them aside also."

He looked at his nurse. "The hospital just called about her X rays. I told them they had made a mistake . . . that they had the wrong person. Now I'm not sure." He was silent for a moment. "Get all of Mrs. Burgio's files and bring them back to my office."

He reached out and pulled me by the arm. "Get in here immediately," he said.

I sat in the examining room waiting for the doctor to finish looking at my files. Finally, he came through the door and closed it behind him.

"I suppose you're going to tell me your MS is healed."

"Right!" I grinned.

"I'll be back in a moment," he said and disappeared through the door again.

When he returned he had me sit on the side of the table while he tapped my knee with his little rubber hammer. There had been little or no knee reflexes for more than ten years. Now my leg jerked at the slightest touch of the hammer.

"I just don't understand," he admitted.

"Do you believe in miracles?" I finally asked.

He looked at me blankly. "No, I don't," he answered.

He stepped back and let his eyes run up and down my body. Once again he checked my reflexes, twisted my arms and legs and listened for long moments with his stethoscope. Folding the instrument, he stuck it in the pocket of his white jacket and leaned against the wall.

"I'm completely baffled," he admitted. "It's as if you had been born again."

"That's it exactly, doctor," I laughed. "I have been born again."

And then I told him the full story of my beautiful miracle healing. He listened patiently, then spoke.

"You've been my patient for thirteen years," he said quietly. "I am so glad for you."

My heart felt a deep twinge of sadness for him as I said, "Doctor, you cared for me all those years—that is true. I could not have asked for better medical care. I will always be grateful to you for that. But you didn't heal me. The Lord did. And the glory for my healing goes to God."

His eyes were serious as he studied my face. I knew that he was a learned medical doctor and that my knowledge was limited, but I also knew I had something he didn't have. He knew it also.

He said thoughtfully, "While I don't understand it, I wish I had a little of whatever it is that you have to give to my other patients."

"All you have to do is reach out, doctor," I said, "and God will touch you also."

His eyes were moist as he took me by the elbow and helped me to the floor from the table. He walked to the door of the examining room with me and lingered for a moment as though he wanted to reach out for more.

"Doctor, is it true that multiple sclerosis is incurable?"

He paused, then answered. "Medically speaking, there is no known cure."

"Is it true that I am healed?"

He nodded his head and gently bit his lower lip. "You are not only healed, Mrs. Burgio; you are a new person!"

"Then to God be the glory," I said. I gave him a little hug, opened the door and walked out into the bright day.

Mr. Benchley was wrong. Life doesn't begin at forty. It begins at fifty-seven!

For Those Who Are Not Healed*

"Why are not *all* healed?" The only honest answer I can give is: I do not know. And I am afraid of those who claim they do know. For only God knows, and who can fathom the mind of God? Who can understand His reasoning?

I think there are some simple matters we can look into, but the ultimate answer as to who is healed and who is not healed lies with God alone.

Often there are those who come praying for physical healing and they get so

---

caught up in the spiritual impact of the miracle service that they forget about their own need. They soon direct their prayers toward others and begin rejoicing over the miracles that take place. Oddly enough, it is often at this precise moment that God chooses to heal—when self is forgotten and God and others come first.

This was what happened for one who had been praying and believing. But others are skeptics—hard-boiled unbelievers in miracles—yet they, too, are often healed. One was healed without ever getting into the service, while there are many who are healed on the way to the service, or while waiting to get in. One woman was healed in her home. One man left shaking his head, not realizing that the Holy Spirit had gone to work in his life and would eventually heal both body and soul. There is no understanding the mind and the ways of Almighty God.

There are thousands and thousands who can prove conclusively that Jesus has healed them and that His power remains the same. The faith that has in times past "subdued kingdoms, wrought righteousness, obtained promises, stopped the mouths of lions, quenched the violence of fire, escaped the edge of the sword . . . turned to flight the armies of the aliens"—*that faith has done it again!*

Yet, we must face facts. There must be a reason why some people are not healed; why there are those who insist that they have "all the faith in the world," and they leave the service in the same condition as when they came. The great tragedy is that discouragements ultimately come with disappointments.

We know from God's Word that a faith that weighs no more than a grain of mustard seed will do more than a ton of will or a mind of determination. The faith that Jesus talked about can no more manifest itself without result than the sun can shine without light and heat. But in many instances people have mistaken their own ability to believe for the faith which only God can give! Faith is not a condition of the mind. It is a divinely imparted grace to the heart.

Our emotions and desires are often mistaken for faith and it is so easy to blame God when there are no results from something that has been purely of the mind and not of the heart. One of the most difficult things in the world is to realize that faith can be received only as it is imparted to the heart by God himself. It cannot be manufactured. No matter how much we nurture and cultivate that spirit the world interprets as faith, it will never grow into the type of faith that was introduced by Jesus.

When we come to our salvation, it is still a matter of faith and, again, He gives us His faith to believe. "As many as received him, to them gave he power to become the sons of God, even to them that believe on his name."

The same Holy Spirit who convicts the sinner of his sin and sees to it that he is given enough conviction to convince him of his sin, will provide faith enough to convince him of his salvation. But no man in himself possesses that faith. It is given him by the same One who gives the faith for our physical healing: the

Author and Finisher of our faith—Christ
Jesus!

With Him there is no struggle! How
often in a miracle service I have seen
conscientious people struggling, straining, demanding that God give them the
healing for their body, and yet there was
no answer.

We can believe in healing. We can
believe in our Lord and His power to
heal. But only Jesus can work the work
that will lift us to the mountain peaks
of victory. We have made faith a product
of a finite mind when all of the other gifts
of the Spirit we have attributed to God.
To many people, faith still is their own
ability to believe a truth, and is often
based on their struggles and their ability
to drive away doubt and unbelief through
a process of continued affirmations.

*There is belief in faith, but faith is
more than belief.* Faith is a gift. Jesus
is our faith, and the Giver of every good
and perfect gift is the Author and Finisher of our faith. Active faith is unquestion-
ing belief, trust and reliance upon God
with all confidence. Faith can become

as real as any of our senses. When we receive His faith we also receive understanding. Everything that God has for His children He puts within the reach of faith. Then He turns around and gives them the faith to appropriate the gift.

Then Jesus spoke. With Him there is no struggle. The waves of doubt and anxiety and worry all fade away and a glorious and marvelous calm and peace enter into the heart and mind of the one who has received that which only He can give. And the only noise will be that of praise and adoration from the lips of the one who has just been healed by the Great Physician.

One of the greatest secrets I have learned through the years is when I have realized my own helplessness and have acknowledged it to Him. It is then that I have experienced some of the greatest manifestations of His power. You are nearest your possession of this imparted grace when you realize your own helplessness and your complete and entire dependence upon the Lord.

I am reminded of the young lady who,

in describing faith, used this illustration. She said, "When I was learning to float on water, I realized I had to relax completely and without fear trust the water to hold me up—it worked, I floated. In the same way I 'faithed.' "

We receive nothing by demanding of God, but it is because of His great love, compassion, and mercy that He gives to us. Often we lose sight of the fact that not one of us can claim any righteousness of our own, not one is worthy of the smallest blessing, but we are the receivers of His blessing because of His mercy and compassion. *Healing is the sovereign act of God.*

When I was twenty years of age, I could have given you all the answers. My theology was straight and I was sure that if you followed certain rules, worked hard enough, obeyed all the commandments, and had yourself in a certain spiritual state, God would heal you.

Lo and behold, my theology came tumbling down and was crushed into a thousand pieces when one day a man who had just entered the auditorium during a miracle service stood silently against the back wall, and after not more than five minutes walked boldly to the stage and freely admitted, "My ear has just opened and I do not believe!"

Although I questioned him repeatedly, he never recanted. Seeing the crowd, out of curiosity he came in, not knowing whether it was an auction or some kind of giveaway program. He was standing there as a spectator and after much questioning I found out that he had not been to church for more than twenty-five years and had put himself in the category of an atheist.

It is possible for me to relate many cases where people have been healed who were amazed, who freely admitted that they did not expect to be healed, who sobbingly cried, "I cannot believe it—I cannot believe it!" Until we have a way of defining it, all that I can tell you is that these are mercy healings. They have been healed through the mercy of the Lord.

We forget the mercy of God, we forget His great compassion, we forget that we do not earn our blessings; neither do we merit His goodness. Were it not for the mercy and the compassion and the grace and the love of God, not one of us would be a Christian. The same holds true when it comes to physical healing. How often I have thought that God cares very little about man's theology, and we are so prone to get dogmatic about things that we know so little about!

God never responds to man's demands to prove Himself. I am amazed at the number of people who try to proposition God. But you cannot put God on the spot; you cannot say to Him, "I am not sure of you, but if you will heal me, then I believe in you."

We have all heard of atheists who have attempted to disprove God by cursing Him and daring Him to strike them dead. Then when nothing happens, they loudly proclaim, "There is no God, else He would have struck back." But God cannot be manipulated.

Jesus recognized this when Satan tempted Him to throw himself from the pinnacle of the Temple and propositioned

God to catch Him up. Satan even quoted scripture to try to prove that God would answer such a presumptuous demand. But you cannot presume upon God. It is up to us to follow God, not demand of Him. *God does not have to prove himself to anyone.*

There are some things in life which will always be unanswerable because we see through a glass darkly. God knows the beginning to the end, while all we can do is catch a glimpse of the present, and a distorted glimpse at that.

If a man like Paul, after all his glorious revelations, did not have the answers for his own thorn in the flesh, then how can we expect to know the answers? God's answer to Paul is adequate to me, "My grace is sufficient for thee: for my strength is made perfect in weakness." Paul's answer to the world should become the password of every believer, "Most gladly, therefore, will I rather glory in my infirmities, that the power of Christ may rest upon me." In Nehemiah's time, when the people were sadly mourning, he said to them,

"The joy of the Lord is your strength." That simply means, *what pleases God is your strength*.

In 1865, when Lincoln was assassinated—the great, patient, mighty Lincoln—an excited throng of thousands gathered in the streets of Washington. They were utterly bewildered, going to and fro as sheep without any shepherd. They were overcome by questions and emotions incident to that tragic hour. But in the midst of the tragic turmoil a man appeared on the steps of the Capitol and said, "God reigns and the government at Washington still lives." The crowds dispersed quietly.

The right words had been said: "*God reigns!*"

OTHER
KATHRYN KUHLMAN
BOOKS
YOU WILL ENJOY

**CAPTAIN LE VRIER BELIEVES
IN MIRACLES**
A Houston police captain is miraculously
healed of incurable cancer.

HOW BIG IS GOD?
A Catholic nurse and all her children are
healed instantly and completely of hopeless
diseases and impairments.

STANDING TALL
The poignant story of a teenage Canadian
girl, tortured by rheumatoid arthritis, who
was miraculously healed by the power of
God.

**TEN THOUSAND MILES
FOR A MIRACLE**
The gripping, true story of Mrs. Morag
McDougall, nearly dead from a series of de-
bilitating heart attacks, and her amazing
healing at a Los Angeles Kathryn Kuhlman
meeting.

Available at
your local bookstore
or from:
BETHANY FELLOWSHIP
6820 Auto Club Road
Minneapolis, MN 55438